AUTISM

FROM A SIBLINGS AND PARENTS PERSPECTIVE

Sarah Yasini

authorHOUSE

AuthorHouse™
1663 Liberty Drive
Bloomington, IN 47403
www.authorhouse.com
Phone: 1 (800) 839-8640

Published by AuthorHouse 12/29/2018

ISBN: 978-1-5462-5826-1 (sc)
ISBN: 978-1-5462-5825-4 (hc)
ISBN: 978-1-5462-5824-7 (e)

Library of Congress Control Number: 2018915307

Print information available on the last page.

CONTENTS

INTRODUCTION

Autism is one of the fastest-growing mental conditions, and it is evident from early childhood. Children with autism often have difficulty communicating, expressing their emotions and creating relationships with peers. Individuals with autism have a difficult life to deal with, but what about the siblings? Why are they always in the background of these tough situations? The parents certainly have a difficult time coping with autism as well, throughout their child's lifespan. In this book, we will look at autism from the perspective of parents and siblings to see what struggles they have and provide some tips for everyone.

PARENT'S PERSPECTIVE

CHAPTER 1

HOW TO EXPLAIN AUTISM TO YOUR CHILDREN

Autism can be a very difficult thing to explain to siblings, especially if they are young and do not understand fully. You should explain it at an early age so they are more mature about it in the future. It is best to open up about it, be honest and explain fully, without oversimplifying it. These are a few tips on how to explain autism to siblings of children with autism.

Be sure to tell them that their sibling loves them. Even if he can't speak, he has love in his heart. He will always be there for them, no matter what, and he will always be by their side. Siblings might not understand at first, and that's okay. Over time, they will see that their sibling with autism is different from them and will figure it out themselves. They may learn from school by experiencing it in special education classes.

As time passes, siblings will understand what autism is and will be more observant toward it. Make sure your child sees her autistic sibling as a person, not just autism; that could ruin the autistic sibling's mental health. Make your children understand why their sibling's behaviour is different, such as why he makes noises, screams or spins around. Tell them that their sibling has a hard time communicating his feelings, resulting in a meltdown.

Children these days are growing up in an environment more accepting of all people, when in the past autistic people were sent to mental asylums. If we raise our children to be kind and accepting, they will treat everyone with kindness and be prepared for the future.

CHAPTER 2

ENCOURAGING CLOSER FAMILY RELATIONSHIPS

Autistic children tend to have an emotional bond with their siblings and parents, which is truly a beautiful thing. Your other children might become jealous that you are spending more time with your autistic child than with them, which can result in lifelong pain and jealousy. Over time, they will understand that their sibling has more needs than they do and that thus their parents have to spend more time with that sibling.

You can encourage closer relationships by doing activities that all your children can enjoy together. According to research, sibling relationships improve when they share activities that all enjoy. It can be quite difficult to choose activities if your children have an age gap or have different interests. For example, if one child wants to play checkers and the other wants to play chess, you can play both at the same time. Make sure to leave your children alone so that they can spend some quality time together and bond more.

Have a therapy session where your children explain to you the frustration and negative feelings they are dealing with, and then explain how they can control it. Build an activity that the whole family can participate in. Focus your attention equally on each child. This will make all your children feel valid and supported. You can even pick out activities where there is a physical activity involved. Try going for a run, swimming or even walking with your children so you all can have fun while also being healthy.

CHAPTER 3

FAMILY DIFFICULTY AND HARDSHIPS

Some families have arguments often, tearing them apart. One parent might not be supportive or care at all, resulting in arguments between parents. Autism can have many negative impacts to the rest of the family, including emotional, marital and sibling.

The emotional impact may be a major one. It may bring joy, frustration or tears. A study in the *Journal of Pediatrics* states that mothers of children with ASD often rated their status of mental health as fair or poor. Compared with the general population, their stress level was much higher. They may feel embarrassment for their child in public and around other family members, such as when the child is having a meltdown. They may have had dreams when they were younger of being the perfect parent, and now they are frustrated when their child turns out to be autistic. They may feel guilt that they are the ones responsible for their child's condition, and they may feel like that for a very long time.

Couples with an autistic child have a 90 percent divorce rate and a 9.7 percent higher chance of divorce than their peers. Reasons for relationship breakups may include a parent denying that a child has autism and simply assuming that the child is bratty or faking it all. A parent may also be violent and sexually or physically abusive with the child. For example, if the child misbehaves, the parent may use harsh discipline because he thinks it will "cure the autism." This may upset other individuals in the family and cause them to hate that parent.

A husband might only see his partner as conceiving autistic children and leave the spouse to start a new family, making life for the single parent extremely difficult. A parent may see his child as a burden to the family, retarded and completely worthless. For siblings, this can be an emotional roller coaster. Siblings who are not diagnosed with an autism spectrum disorder (ASD) may feel stress from their home life and not be able to keep up with their social and school lives. The parents' attention might be completely focused on the autistic sibling, thus making them feel left out and neglected. Furthermore, they might feel that they don't fit in at school since their friends don't have autistic siblings, and they will feel angry if someone makes a joke about autism.

Finally, there is the financial impact. In many countries, such as the United States, there is no free health care. Doctor appointments can cost over $200. Many families struggle to keep up with the bills. Having a child with autism may also require a parent to leave her job so she can take care of the child, leaving only one breadwinner in the house. Many children diagnosed with ASD take medication on a daily basis, which is also very expensive. It can cost between $50 to $1,000 for one month of medication.

CHAPTER 4

VIOLENCE AND AGGRESSION

Aggressive behaviour in autistic individuals may start as young as three years old. They may be aggressive toward themselves, which is called *self-injurious behaviour*. This may include hitting, kicking, throwing objects or headbanging. There are a number of reasons why they behave like this, one being trouble understanding what is going on around them and not being able to communicate. As a parent, you should look for and understand what triggers your child's behaviour and try to prevent it. You can try to look at it as an ABC sandwich:

- **Antecedents**—These are what triggers your child's aggressive and self-injurious behaviour.
- **Behaviour**—The way your child reacts to the triggers.
- **Consequences**—This is what your child gets from behaving aggressively.

The best thing to do during a meltdown is to stay as calm as you can. When you stay calm and don't get angry, you are able to handle the situation better. If your child is hitting himself, it's best to restrain him.

Try putting a helmet on him to prevent him from severely injuring himself. If you have paintings or glass anywhere in your home, get rid of it immediately. By leaving unsafe objects around the house, you create a situation where your child may easily pick one up and injure himself or you.

It is best to keep the siblings out of this situation so they don't get hurt. A family can be deeply impacted by autism aggression, and these bad memories will haunt them throughout their lifetime. Autistic children physically and emotionally hurt their families when they have meltdowns. They can even break a few bones when they have violent meltdowns.

CHAPTER 5

BLAME

Your children might blame themselves for your stress, and that can take a serious toll on their mental health. As stated earlier, couples who have an autistic child have a 90 percent divorce rate, and oftentimes the child with autism blames himself for his parents' separation and thinks that his autism is breaking up the family.

Autistic individuals shouldn't blame themselves in any way; autism is no one's fault. I used to blame myself for my brother's autism, and he also blamed himself. Society also blames the autistic individual for whatever happens, such as the Toronto van attack, in which the suspect possibly had an autism spectrum disorder. I hate to see autism identified as a relevant factor in an episode of violence, because it implies that people should be afraid of boys like my brother.

CHAPTER 6

MEDICATION

While medication is useful and some kids do take it, it might not be healthy for the brain. It does usually work for children, but in some cases, it can take a negative toll on them. You should do research on medications so that your child can use them safely and carefully. Your health care professional should explain the medication to you, including what it is used for, any side effects, ways to tell that it's effective and the benefits hoped for. If the medication doesn't work immediately, give it time; it usually starts taking effect in a couple of weeks or months.

When my brother first took Prozac to treat his anxiety, it absolutely had a severe negative impact on his brain and body. He began drinking up to twenty cups of water a day because his mouth felt dry. His obsessive-compulsive disorder became worse, and his heartbeat was faster than normal. One time, we almost had to take him to the hospital.

Once we stopped the Prozac, my brother became better and healthier. The Prozac almost killed him, but we are happy that God helped us and my brother. However, just because medication didn't work for my brother, that doesn't mean it won't work for your child.

·

CHAPTER 7

MENTAL HEALTH AND AUTISM

Research has found that over 80 percent of autistic individuals have mental health problems, including anxiety, depression and obsessive-compulsive disorder. Anxiety is very common amongst individuals on the autism spectrum. About 40 percent are reported to have anxiety, compared with just 15 percent of the population. Individuals may have anxiety attacks from time to time, and it's best to keep calm in such a situation. There are ways to treat anxiety disorders, one of which is talking it out. With a therapist, patients can work on a set of challenges they can improve on one step at a time.

According to *Psychology Today*, depressed autistic youth were twenty-eight times more likely to attempt suicide than typical children. In some cases, you cannot tell if the person has depression because of how well the individual functions, both emotionally and physically. Some signs of depression are sudden eating changes, eating too little or too much or crying too much.

Autistic people who are verbal may tell you how they feel emotionally, so it's best to get them help right away. If you feel as if your child will commit suicide, or if your child has attempted suicide, it is best to offer support and be there for them at tough times. Be there for your child and listen to what they have to stay or be there to comfort them. Try to understand their perspective and what they are going through.

Consider writing a safety plan for the person to use if suicidal thoughts return. It may include calling the suicide hotline, calling you or someone the person feels close to or trying things to become more calm, such as taking a shower or drinking cold water.

CHAPTER 8

TRYING NEW FOODS

When children are young and developing, parents decide what is healthy for the child's development. Many children at a very young age are picky eaters, and most of them hate vegetables and love junk food. They usually grow out of this when they are older, but for children on the autism spectrum, the eating problem is much more severe. Parents get little to no medical help with the eating habits; doctors think that the child will grow out of it.

Some signs that your child may have an eating problem include eating only liquid foods; choking and gagging when seeing or tasting food; loss of oxygen when eating; spitting out the food and refusing to eat; and having excess food come out of their nostrils. Children with autism may also take an interest in eating non-edible food—such as paper, dirt or plastic—so it's best to keep them away from these things.

To help your child eat nutritious food, try blending in new foods with the food they usually eat. For example, if they eat pasta, add a little cheese inside the pasta. It may become a new favourite food!

You can also play with the food and make it more fun. Try carving out a smiley face on some fruit or use cookie cutters to cut fun shapes on some foods. There are also doctors who specialize in eating who may be able to help children with autism improve their eating habits.

CHAPTER 9

SCHOOL AND POSTSECONDARY

Most autistic children tend to be in special education classrooms with other autistic children, but they may face difficulties with communication, social skills and sensory sensitivity. Many parents choose to homeschool or take their child out of school entirely because their child can't handle the stress of school.

According to CBS News, over 63 percent of autistic individuals are bullied in school, and this has doubled in recent years. They are more prone to bullying if they are in a regular classroom because the other students think they are weird and unusual. Many come home feeling upset that they have been bullied and wondering what is wrong with them. Transitioning to high school may be a different and scary turning point for autistic youth.

At school, things can be quite challenging. Autistic children tend to hit and throw objects in the classroom and abuse their classmates. Some autistic youth have sensory problems, meaning their ears are very sensitive and they can't tolerate loud or screeching noises. If their classmate perhaps accidentally screeches a chair, it can result in a meltdown. Some schoolteachers abuse children with autism. Take the clover teachers, for example, or the police officer who handcuffed the little boy who was having a tantrum.

With all these challenges, school can be very difficult for individuals with autism, and those difficulties should not be taken lightly. If your child is struggling in school, it's best to switch to homeschooling. Recently, my brother has been following a homeschooling program, and it has had a positive impact on his life. He didn't like public schools very much, and my mother often had to pick him up because he was throwing a tantrum. Homeschooling is better for him; he can learn in the comfort of his own home, and he is happy with my mom and me helping him with his coursework.

CHAPTER 10

GROUP HOMES

One of the hardest things for families of children with autism is not being able to take care of these children as young adults and eventually sending them to a group home. There are pros and cons to group homes. Let's start with the pros first.

The first pro is that sending a family member with autism to a group home helps the rest of the family cope with their lives. Taking care of an autistic child can be very difficult and emotionally draining. As the children get older, the parents age as well and are not able to take care of the autistic family member very well. Siblings may have moved on with their lives and are too busy to take care of their sibling.

Another pro of group homes is that individuals may feel more independent there than in their actual house. In a group home, they have responsibilities they take care of. Each resident has a task to do each day. They feel that they have worked hard and are living a good lifestyle.

A con is the trust you have to put in the home personnel to keep your child safe. We all know that physical abuse happens, even in group homes. A worker might tend to abuse individuals with special needs if they don't do something right or if the worker doesn't have the skill to cope with their behavioural issues. Group homes are also very expensive, especially to those who have financial struggles.

Now I will share my experience with abuse in a group home. My mom's friend's kids all have autism, and one is in a group home. One day, he was in the park with his supervisors who were watching him, and he started to have a meltdown. Instead of being mature and an actual adult in the situation, a supervisor abused him, slapping and kicking him. The supervisor told him that he shouldn't tell anyone, but fortunately, he did. The police came and eventually arrested the abuser. It can be very difficult to find a reliable group home.

CHAPTER 11

MANAGING STRESS

A family member with autism brings a lot of stress for parents and siblings. Stress can take a negative toll on your life or even take over your whole life. One way to handle it is to make time for yourself doing your favourite activities. Try reading a book, meditating (yoga) or just simply catching up on some sleep.

Another way to combat stress is to seek support from friends and family, and stop only relying on yourself. Therapy might help, but there is much more to it than just sharing your feelings. Whether it's a friend, a family member, a support group, a therapist or an autism specialist, it is up to you to seek out the help you need.

Finally, aspire to personal growth for yourself and your child. One way parents can ensure that they take care of their kids effectively is to take care of themselves first, both emotionally and physically. You don't want to take your anger out on your children, so it's best to manage your stress. There are stress-management activities that you and your child can do together, such as art, music and hydrotherapy.

For art therapy, you can bring out your child's favourite colouring book, and you can both colour peacefully together. You can also paint together, as painting minimizes muscle soreness, joint pain and headaches. As for music therapy, if your child has sensory problems or doesn't like music, you can listen to the sounds of nature. A recommendation is to listen to the sound of rain. It soothes your mind and makes you feel calmer.

For hydrotherapy, you and your child can both go in a swimming pool and have a nice swim together. If your child doesn't like to go swimming in a pool, you can take a nice shower—both of you or just you. A hot shower is recommended because it relaxes muscles, adjusts body temperature and calms the brain.

CHAPTER 12

ACTIVITIES AND SPORTS

Some autistic children enjoy participating in sports and activities, but others do not. Team sports, such as soccer or basketball, may not be a good choice for your child. Playing on a team requires advanced social communication skills. Autism is a disorder in which those skills are compromised. So it can be tough for autistic kids to fit into a team, communicate well with other team members or find out what another team member is likely to do in a game.

Individual private sports are best, such as swimming, bowling or track and field. Swimming is an easy sport that requires no ball passing, only fun water play and different strokes. Bowling is also a wonderful sport and very fun to play. Autistic children are very satisfied when the pins come down. It is not a tiring sport and has many breaks.

Physical activity is very good for the brain and body, so everyone should do it at least one hour a day. In the US, more than 16 percent of children ages 2 to 19 are overweight. The numbers are even higher for kids diagnosed with ASD, with 19 percent being overweight and over 36 percent at risk. Obesity problems may lead to other health issues as well, such as diabetes and bone and joint problems.

I conducted an experiment with ten people over the course of one month involving physical activity and mental health improvement. Five people did thirty minutes of hard physical activity a day, and five people did one hour of light exercise.

In a span of one month, it turned out that the people who did one hour of light exercise had better results. The people with a thirty-minute workout routine commented that their overall fitness and stamina improved and they lost two to eight pounds, but they felt tired daily and experienced muscle pain. The individuals who did the light exercises had improved flexibility overall. They felt that their mental health had improved, and they lost between two and five pounds that month. This study concluded that the people who did thirty minutes of exercise did lose more weight, but the other individuals' mental health improved.

I did another experiment in which individuals worked out six days a week: three days of hard workouts and three days of light workouts, both one hour a day. To my surprise, this had a more positive outcome than the other experiment. The participants felt that their mental health and physical health improved tremendously and recommended that everyone try it.

CHAPTER 13

PUBERTY

Puberty is a tough time in every teenager's life, but it can be even harder on autistic teens. For boys, puberty includes facial-hair growth, a deeper voice and getting taller and stronger. For girls, it includes their menstrual cycle, developing breasts and hair growth in areas like the armpits. It is important for parents to talk to their children about these changes before they happen so the children will know about it more and take care of themselves.

You can use a set of images or cartoons if your child is a visual learner or non-verbal. For menstruation, it is best to teach your daughter about it before she starts getting it so she doesn't get scared when it happens. Teach her what a pad and a tampon are and how to use each one. It is best to use a pad first rather than a tampon, as a pad is easier to use and a tampon goes inside you.

As for sexual feelings, they may cause anxiety and confusion in autistic children. Your child may masturbate, which is a completely healthy thing to do, and it also lets out sexual tension. You should teach your child when it is appropriate to masturbate and when it is not. You can also get your therapist to talk about it with your child if your child feels uncomfortable talking about such things with you.

Your child may have sexual feelings about and crushes on the opposite gender and might want to be in a relationship. Unfortunately, many autistic youth have a hard time communicating, and so having a partner is extremely difficult for them. People with autism have the right to be in a relationship and engage in sexual activity, but society blocks them from relationships. It is best to explain sex at the start of puberty, so they will understand why they are having sexual feelings. It is best to not just jump in right at sexual intercourse but to take things slowly.

An appropriate start is to teach children with autism about safe touch and dangerous touch. Teach them to never sexually touch others without permission. Teach them about consent and the privacy of their own body. If you take small steps, your child will have the best sexual education and be more knowledgeable in the area.

After that, teach children about personal hygiene. This includes brushing their teeth two to four times a day, taking showers whenever they are dirty and using deodorant. You can go shopping together for deodorant and let your child choose the scent. This will make it more exciting to use.

Finally, talk about the changes that their body is going through. Breast development, hair growth and penis growth are important subjects to talk about. Next, talk about the genitalia—in other words, the penis and the vagina. You can draw diagrams of what these look like so your child will have a visual to look at.

Unfortunately, with puberty comes aggression, if it is not already a problem. Individuals diagnosed with ASD often become aggressive during puberty, and it might be mild or severe. The aggression might stop when children are 18 or 19 years old, because that is when they reach adulthood. Their body stops changing and is fully developed.

CHAPTER 14

FUTURE HOPES AND PLANS

A parent's first thought when a child is diagnosed with autism is, "What will happen in the future?" You may be worried about who is going to look after your child when you die. It may be a sibling or another family member, but these people might not be able to take care of your child because they have roles and responsibilities of their own to take care of. It is best to plan for the future now instead of waiting for the future to arrive.

The future is unknown for an individual with autism. There are many factors that will influence their lives, both negatively and positively. For now, you should enjoy the life you have with your kids and spend more time with them. Parents usually worry about how their child will manage life as an adult, if there will be a need for support and how their child will be financially secure. Parents also struggle finding a group home for their child and worry if it's trustworthy and if the workers will do their jobs well. Steps to prepare for the future include the following:

- **Creating a life plan.** This includes all your plans for education, housing, monthly food costs, medical care and leisure activities.
- **Choose a type of housing.** Decide on where your child will live. It may be a group home, with siblings or in his or her own home.

- **Do your research.** Find out about disability benefits, life insurance, savings and government benefits.
- **Share your plan with others.** Review your plans with family members and have them keep a record.

CHAPTER 15

NOT YOUR FAULT

Many parents believe that it's their fault they have an autistic child. This is not true; why would it be your fault? Autism is a condition that happens for no reason. There is no need to blame yourself. It's also not your doctor's or your family's fault either.

Many people say to parents that "Your child has autism because he is bratty" or "Your child has autism because you don't take good care of him." The truth is you can't make a child autistic by spoiling them or treating them badly. Often when parents first hear doctors diagnosing a child with autism spectrum disorder, they have a variety of emotions. These can range from anger and frustration to sadness and confusion. It's easy to want to blame someone at that time. Remember, however, that parents help their children with problems, and you will always be there for your child. Don't let negative emotions get to you.

If you're feeling guilt and frustration, know that it will get better. One day you will look back and think all the tears and frustration were worth it. Try talking to a therapist or someone you love about your negative emotions. Remember that you are not responsible for your child getting autism. Take time to relax and take care of yourself.

CHAPTER 16

VACCINES

There have been many reports that vaccines cause autism, but is it true? It depends on your personal opinion. Mine is yes, that vaccines do cause autism. Many parents have been concerned about this controversial topic, and many have spoken up and protested against it. Vaccines have also been tested on animals several times, and each one of them had signs of autism in days. Meanwhile, other studies have concluded that vaccines do not cause autism.

One vaccine ingredient, thimerosal, contains mercury to prevent contamination. Thousands of mothers have shared their stories on the MMR vaccine and how it gave their child autism in a matter of days. There is another substance in vaccines that may be linked to autism, and that is human DNA. Human DNA can cause brain damage because the vaccine is being injected into a human, and that can cause the body to kill brain tissue.

Everyone has their own opinion on the vaccine and autism link, but many studies have concluded that it doesn't exist. Vaccines do keep you from getting certain diseases, which is a positive point, and they stop the spreading of diseases.

CHAPTER 17

AUTISM IN SECOND AND THIRD WORLD COUNTRIES

Living in a Second or Third World country and having a child with autism is a very big struggle. In many parts of Asia, such as Afghanistan, many do honour killings of those who have put shame to their family name, including children with special needs. They are often called retarded by their parents, or the disorder is overlooked as the child just being a brat.

Many countries don't have the services we have in Canada and the United States—such as therapists, doctors or psychologists—resulting in confusion as to why the child is acting this way. When I went to Afghanistan, Pakistan and India, children with special needs were ridiculed and shamed. When they walked down the street, people stared, pointed and laughed. It got to the point where they were even beaten on the streets by neighbourhood bullies and sexually, emotionally and physically abused by their parents and siblings.

The police are useless in these countries. Many don't care and don't take these types of abuse seriously. In parts of Africa, such as Kenya, abuse is present too. An article describes a 4-year old Kenyan boy who was not doing well in school, so his teachers beat him excessively. In parts of Africa, youngsters with autism "are labeled as devils, are not diagnosed, and not given treatment." The situation is not very good in First or Second World countries either. Special needs individuals are labeled as "useless to society" and "retarded."

CHAPTER 18

SOCIETY

Society has negative words and feelings for certain people, including people with autism. Autistic individuals face discrimination in many settings, including school, work and even at home. At school, kids get bullied for being autistic, and people often make jokes about them. If we teach our children to be accepting of others, no matter their race, religion or disability, we can change the world and make it more of a diverse place. Being autistic isn't something that someone should have to be ashamed about. It's not something that should be used to discriminate against people, and not something that should keep others from disclosing for fear of how they'll be viewed by society.

As for work, companies might not hire people because they are autistic and might not think they have the skills to work there. At home, parents might see their child as nothing or blaming them for the negatives in their lives, as society tells them. Society also tells autistic individuals that they should be grateful that someone is being nice to them, but shouldn't you be nice to all people?

People with autism do not have recognizable facial features like people with Down syndrome. They're not in a wheelchair, so their disability is not easily recognized. If your child is having a meltdown in public, strangers may ask you to control your child. Maybe they blame you for not disciplining your child, or they might know he has autism but blame you for not controlling him. To combat this, educate people about what autism is, what you have experienced and the stigma around it. Participate in autism conferences in your location, and join autism awareness committees and clubs.

CHAPTER 19

CLOTHES

Some autistic people struggle with clothing, whether wearing it or being picky about it. Some refuse to wear new clothes and instead wear the same clothes every day. Many autistic individuals struggle with undergarments, such as underwear, bras and boxers. They aren't used to the change during puberty when girls need to wear bras, or needing to wear underwear when you don't wear diapers anymore.

Autistic people who can't communicate verbally may use certain noises to say they don't want to wear the clothes or refuse to wear them. The friction or fabric of underwear may feel uncomfortable to your child, and that is totally fine. They need some time to get used to wearing undergarments, so be patient with them.

Autistic individuals are sometimes picky with their choice of clothing, whether it be the colour, company or style. Clothes shopping can be long and difficult.

CHAPTER 20

LOVE OR HATE?

Most parents who have autistic children love their kids, no matter how frustrated and stressed they get. They want the best for their kids and will make sacrifices to keep their child happy, even if they are not.

However, there are parents who do not love their autistic children but rather despise them. In many recent books about autism, parents are the narrators and say horrific things to their children. There are many ways to damage your child without even knowing about it, such as talking about them while they are in the room, assuming that autism is their whole personality and teaching them that their autism is a bad thing.

First, talking about them while they are in the room with you can damage their emotions, especially if you are saying negative things. You may talk about how your life is difficult raising them or how much they have ruined your life. Even if they are non-verbal, that doesn't mean they can't hear what you are saying about them. They hear everything and may have mixed emotions about their parents.

Assuming that autism is your child's entire identity is also something that should be avoided. Autism is not all there is to a person. Individuals with autism have a life and activities they enjoy despite their condition.

Finally, teaching children that autism is a bad thing can ruin their lives. They will constantly think that they are a burden to their family because of their condition and that they should have never been born.

Many autistic children are physically and sexually abused by their parent or parents. Physical abuse includes punching, slapping, kicking, shaking, biting and burning which is not accidental. Sexual abuse includes an individual being molested and non-consensual sex against their will.

There are signs to look for in identifying abuse, such as weight loss, isolation and avoiding particular people and places. If you know that your loved one is being abused, call law enforcement immediately. It is also best to educate your children about warning signs of abuse. You should tell them to be honest and open about their feelings and if they are in crisis.

CHAPTER 21

SUICIDE IN PARENTS

Committing suicide while you have an autistic child is probably one of the most selfish things a human can do. The child will now have only one parent or become an orphan. Children will blame themselves for their parent's suicide and have hatred for themselves and their condition. These parents left their autistic children in the world with one parent or no one else to take care of them. Imagine the abuse those children will face.

Yet people feel compassion for the parent instead of the child, saying things like "The mother must have struggled a lot" or "They wanted a normal child." Those are some of the most ridiculous things I have ever heard. Of course you are going to have struggles raising an autistic child, and you had a dream of having a normal, happy family, but this child will be the best person you have ever known and will love ever so deeply. If you are having suicidal thoughts, please get help right away. Call the suicide hotline. If you see warning signs of a suicidal person, get help immediately.

CHAPTER 22

DELAYED DEVELOPMENT

Every person on the spectrum is different. No two are alike, just like snowflakes. But one thing that is rarely talked about is developmental delays in autism. A typical child begins walking at 9 months old; a child with developmental delays may walk at 17 to 19 months. Delayed development may also affect how a child acts and what the child's behaviour is typically like. A 15-year-old male with autism may act like an 8-year-old boy and not like a mature teenager. The brain is slower at developing, causing those with developmental delays to grow up and mature more slowly. Children with developmental delays may need help with showering, getting ready for the day and toilet training.

When my brother was just 2 years old, my family realized he was not developing like other children his age. He was non-verbal until he was 4 years old and started speaking fully when he was 8. He also did not respond to sounds, and when we called his name, he acted like we weren't there. He was not eating solid foods until he was 9 years old; instead, he ate mashed-up foods. He has diagnosed with developmental delays and autism. He still has developmental delays, but he is conquering that every day.

Some signs of developmental concerns include the following:

- not speaking at a certain age
- difficulty eating
- difficulty with school and trying to understand the lesson
- not walking or attempting to walk

CHAPTER 23

ELECTRONICS

Children with autism have a higher rate of being addicted to electronics and video games. I will share my personal story about video games and electronics addiction. My brother has autism, and my parents bought him an iPad when he was 10 years old and a video game console when he was 8 years old. I knew it was a bad idea, and I told my parents not to buy these for him, but they insisted.

For the next few months, he was playing video games for 12 hours a day, never stopping, and eating in the same room where he was playing. The video games took a very negative toll on his brain; he was dizzy all the time, became more violent and was extremely antisocial. He was addicted for about five years; then, at age 13, he just stopped and started hating video games. I don't know why he suddenly stopped out of the blue, but it was a good thing. Since then, he has developed in a positive way and spends more time with us.

CHAPTER 24

THE GOOD DOCTOR

The Good Doctor is a show that debuted on television in September 2017. It is about a surgeon who has autism and savant syndrome, making him a genius. Throughout the show, we see his struggle with autism as he works at a prestigious hospital with a few arrogant patients and staff members.

What is very important about this show is that it features an autistic character who is not just in the background but the main character. Individuals with autism are often mistreated. People say they can't have good jobs and are too stupid, but this character with autism is a genius.

This is one of my favourite shows, mainly because it features an autistic character, which I never saw growing up. The main point of the show is that even if you do have autism, it doesn't define you as a person. You can follow your dreams and live your best life.

CHAPTER 25

PHOBIAS

All humans are scared of something, and people with autism are no exception. Individuals with autism tend to be scared of unusual things, not typical fears such as arachnophobia (fear of spiders) or acrophobia (fear of heights). Some phobias and strong dislikes include loud noises, touch and crowded areas (claustrophobia).

For loud noises, they may hear a screech from a chair and cover their ears or have a meltdown. That's why it's a good idea to have children with autism wear noise-blocking headphones if they have sensory issues. As for touch, they may not like parts of their body touched or only trust their loved ones. In crowded areas, they may not like touching shoulders with another person or not like being in a tight space for a long period of time, such as a car ride.

These phobias might go away over time, or they might last a lifetime, but there are many ways to reduce them. One is participating in clubs where autistic individuals can develop communication skills and heal their fear of speaking. Another is finding a therapist to help your child overcome these phobias, with baby steps along the way.

CHAPTER 26

SPEECH AND NON-VERBAL

Autistic individuals may have a speech problem from an early age. Some may be non-verbal and make noises such as shrieks and grunts; others may talk normally but with a few problems. Individuals with autism may talk about a favourite topic for a long period of time, or it might be the only topic they talk about.

From my personal experience, I know many autistic people who speak of the same topic almost every day and never talk about anything else. My brother talks about cars for up to twelve hours a day, and my friend talks about her brother all day when we are at school.

Speech therapy is one solution and has improved many lives, including mine. Speech language pathologists are therapists who treat communication problems and speech disorders. Parents should keep in mind that this is a very important process in autism therapy. Speech pathologists will assess the best way to improve communication and enhance a child's quality of life. The speech pathologist will closely work with the family, the school and other professionals. In some cases, if the child is having major trouble with speech, the speech pathologist may introduce alternatives to speech.

CHAPTER 27

SAME ROUTINE

Autistic people have almost the same routine every day, and most are not accustomed to changes in their daily routine. For an individual with autism, our world is truly an unpredictable place. Many children, including my brother, have a routine similar to this: wake up in the morning, go to the washroom and brush teeth, put on clothes, eat breakfast, put on outdoor wear and get ready to go to school or any other planned activity. They might do their daily routine at the same time as well, such as eating breakfast at nine o'clock. People with autism are naturally determined to repeat their routines, which can result in consistent routines monthly and yearly.

If you want to change your child's daily routine, it's best to take baby steps instead of doing it all at once, since your child is not used to the sudden change. Sometimes it is best if your child does have a routine, because it reduces stress and makes the day easier for parents. Your child should have a routine during mealtime, such as the following:

- Wash hands thoroughly with soap and water.
- Sit at the table and say prayers.
- Eat meal and finish all the food on the plate.
- Help clean up the table when done.

It is also best for children with autism to have a bedtime routine, so they can go to bed early and not make it a difficult situation. Your child's bedtime routine may go as follows:

- Take a shower or bath; it should be short and not last too long.
- Put on pyjamas.
- Floss, brush teeth and use mouthwash.
- Listen to a bedtime story, or just go to sleep in one's own room.

CHAPTER 28

SERVICE ANIMALS

Service animals are great for autistic individuals. They help these individuals in their daily routine and when they are in need of assistance or in crisis. Many individuals with autism have trouble with empathy, but studies show that children with autism with service dogs have more empathy than children who don't have service dogs.

The children see their dog as a peer rather than a pet. These dogs are helpful in a variety of ways; they can help children improve social interactions and relationships, increase verbal and non-verbal communication, learn life skills and have increased interest in activities. The dogs also help decrease stress within the family.

Service dogs can protect the individual from harm, so parents can ensure that their child is always safe when going out alone. Service animals can also become the child's companion. Even my friend who hated dogs in the past found a service animal beneficial. He didn't like to be around dogs, but he needed a service dog to help him with daily routines and to protect him from harm. He almost instantly adapted to the dog, and they became best friends. No matter what, if you have a dog, it will be your best friend forever.

CHAPTER 29

TOILET TRAINING

It is certainly difficult for a parent to teach an autistic child how to use the toilet and get out of diapers. The child will get it eventually, but it will take time and effort. Some autistic individuals lack the communication skills to tell their parents that they need to use the toilet or don't have the physical ability to use a toilet, making the task extremely difficult. Some may be interested in doing other activities at the toilet rather than doing their business, such as flushing, playing with the water of the toilet and not sitting long enough on the toilet.

There are many solutions to this, and I will share some of my own. For children who like to play with the water in the toilet, get them to play with water in a cleaner and different area of your house, such as your sink. Your child will adapt to this and stop playing with the toilet water. You should also teach your child to only flush once after using the toilet. Let your child do the flushing while you watch.

If your child does not want to sit on the toilet seat, you can be a leader and demonstrate how to sit. You can also bring a favourite stuffed animal as a tool to teach your child how to sit. Use visuals to educate your child about toilet training or even put on a video or a cartoon.

CHAPTER 30

DEATH OF A CHILD

The risk of premature death is 2.5 times higher for people diagnosed with autism spectrum disorder than the rest of the population. There are three main causes of premature death for autistic people, one of which is suicide. When a child commits suicide, the parents blame themselves for not helping more or noticing that their child was depressed.

A second major cause of death for individuals on the autism spectrum is epilepsy. Epilepsy is a common neurological disorder that often results in diagnosed individuals having unpredictable seizures. A person can die from epilepsy if seizures cause brain damage, if a seizure lasts too long or if a seizure causes inhaling problems, such as choking on one's own vomit.

Finally, heart problems and cancer are also a cause for premature death. The survival rate for cancer is low, but some individuals do survive.

The death of a child can be very hard on a parent, and everything in your house will bring back memories of your child. It is best to tell your relatives about your child's death. They will support you in getting better. Don't let the media be involved in the death case; they will only make it more stressful and frustrating.

CHAPTER 31

HOW TO HELP A PARENT WHO HAS AN AUTISTIC CHILD

If you know a parent who is raising a child with autism, always be there for them, no matter what obstacles get in the way. Always support and love the parents, and tell them that things will get better. Here are some ways to help parents who have an autistic child:

1. **Talk about feelings.** Parents should never hold their feelings inside. It will cause them stress, and eventually they will lash out at their child. Always listen to what the parent is saying, and provide support and comfort.

2. **Learn about autism spectrum disorder.** Learning about autism can provide better knowledge and understanding of how the parents are feeling.

3. **Accept.** Most people have a hard time accepting that a child has autism. They think that the child will grow out of it or is just bratty. If more people came to understand autism as a serious condition, there would be more acceptance in the world.

4. **Offer babysitting.** Oftentimes, parents of autistic children cannot find a babysitter, simply because babysitters can't cope with an autistic child. You can help! If the parents wants a break to relax or have a date night, you can babysit the child

for the night. This will help you gain experience in taking care of children while also having a fun time.

5. **Offer friendship.** Most of the time, autistic individuals have a hard time making friends due to their communication skills. Friends are very important to have in your life, for the sake of emotional and mental well-being. If you have children, you can help them become friends with the child with autism, so that child doesn't feel lonely.

CHAPTER 32

HOW AUTISM AND DOWN SYNDROME ARE CONNECTED

Autism and Down syndrome have many similarities, but they also have their differences. Some individuals are diagnosed with both autism and Down syndrome. You can tell people have Down syndrome because they have the same facial features, but autism is not recognizable.

What is Down syndrome? It's a genetic condition that causes delays in physical and intellectual development. Individuals have one extra chromosome—47 instead of the usual 46. There are three types of Down syndrome:

- **Trisomy 21:** About 95 percent of people with Down syndrome have trisomy 21. With this type of Down syndrome, each cell in the body has three separate copies of chromosome 21 instead of the usual two copies.
- **Translocation Down syndrome:** This type accounts for a small percentage of people with Down syndrome (about 3 percent). This occurs when an extra part or a whole extra chromosome 21 is present, but it is attached or "translocated" to a different chromosome rather than being a separate chromosome 21.
- **Mosaic Down syndrome:** This type affects about 2 percent of people with Down syndrome. *Mosaic* means "mixture" or "combination." For children with mosaic Down syndrome,

some of their cells have three copies of chromosome 21 rather than the usual two. Children with mosaic Down syndrome may have the same but fewer features as other children with Down syndrome.

Characteristics of Down Syndrome

Behavioural characteristics:

- language impairment
- impulsiveness
- short attention span
- sensory issues
- aggression
- self-abuse
- refusing to comply with requests
- picky eating

Physical characteristics:

- flattened face, especially the bridge of the nose
- almond-shaped eyes that slant up
- short neck
- tongue that tends to stick out of the mouth
- small hands and feet
- poor muscle tone or loose joints
- shorter in height as children and adults

Similarities to autism include aggression, self-abuse, sensory issues and language impairment.

CHAPTER 33

WANTING A PARTNER

When we reach puberty, we see ourselves being attracted to the opposite sex, having crushes and wanting to be in a relationship. For people with autism, being in a relationship is harder than for a typical person. They don't have the proper communication skills to go talk to someone and may seem awkward at times. Sometimes they want to be in a relationship because they want to feel normal for a change and like typical people.

Getting a partner most likely will require investing a lot of time and effort in learning the social skills of relationships—how to flirt, how to read someone's body language, how to make someone feel loved and desired. Most of these things autistic people have learned the hard way by trial and error. They need to get comfortable and spend time with others, get comfortable asking people out, get comfortable with rejection, get enough self-esteem to seem desirable and be able to handle the ups and downs without beating themselves up too much.

Here are some ways for people with autism to get a girlfriend or boyfriend:

- Go to blind-date groups
- Be themselves; don't be someone they're not.
- Ask friends or loved ones for help if they are struggling or confused about something.

CHAPTER 34

JOYS OF HAVING A CHILD WITH AUTISM

You can learn a lot from your child and see the world in a different light. You get to see your child developing through childhood and adulthood and forming relationships with people such as yourself, doctors, babysitters and teachers.

My brother has developed quite the sense of humour. When I tell amusing stories or talk about my funniest and most embarrassing moments, I can always count on him to get a good laugh out of it.

It's all about having hope and never saying never. We always count on God to make our struggles better and hope that my brother will get better. I will always remember his accomplishments and how hard he tries to overcome his challenges. I will take that over anything else.

SIBLING'S PERSPECTIVE

CHAPTER 35

SCHOOL LIFE

Individuals who have a sibling with autism often feel uncomfortable in school. They think of their sibling's well-being while they are in school, and sometimes they have difficulty concentrating. Their teachers and friends often don't understand what hardships are going on in their life, putting them at a higher risk for depression and suicide. Many have left school because they have to take care of their sibling after the death of their parents.

Sometimes they have to deal with people bullying and teasing their sibling and have to stand up for their brother or sister. They are sometimes embarrassed around their friends and don't mention that their sibling has autism, in fear of being targeted for bullying. They have to encounter the many jokes about autism that are spread around school, making them feel alone in the world and that they have no one who understands how difficult it is to live with an autistic person.

Over the years, I have learned to cope with the number of autism jokes I hear at school, and it doesn't affect me anymore. Remember— others' negativity should not rub off on you. You love your sibling no matter what. Don't listen to what people tell you.

CHAPTER 36

RELATIONSHIPS

Many people, when they are going through puberty, find themselves attracted to the opposite sex they once called gross. While 38 percent of teens are now in relationships, youth who have autistic siblings do not fall under that percentage. Many do not have time to do the activities they wish because they have to stay home taking care of their sibling.

Some may also not be in relationships because they are worried about caregiving in the future when their parents pass away. Your sibling might also not want you to get a partner out of fear that you will drift away. Remind your sibling that boyfriends and girlfriends come and go, but siblings are forever.

Here are some tips for introducing your sibling to the person you are dating:

- Start talking about your boyfriend or girlfriend around the house to your parents so your sibling will catch on.
- Help your sibling find a social life. It is very difficult if your sibling wants a boyfriend or girlfriend, since people with autism often lack the proper communication skills to go pursue someone. There are a few places where autistic individuals can go and meet other autistic individuals and get a better

understanding of the dating life. You can also explain dating to your sibling if you or someone you know has a partner.

- Introduce your boyfriend or girlfriend to your sibling. Your sibling may have a surprised reaction at first but will get used to it later on.

CHAPTER 37

STRENGTHS OF AUTISTIC PEOPLE

Many people talk about the negatives of individuals with autism. Now let's talk about the positives. One strength is that they are usually very skilled in a certain area, such as art, music and dancing. For my brother, it's automobiles. He can name every car company on the planet and every single part of a car.

Another strength is great attention to detail, and it comes in handy if you have missed an important detail yourself. Most autistic individuals have average to higher intelligence than typical people. Most are very honest and tell it like it is, which is sometimes a negative and sometimes a positive. They also will have a conversation with you without judging you for what you are saying, unlike most people.

Autistic people rarely judge others, which is a big problem in society, since we constantly judge each other. They are more accepting of differences, and many of them have gone on to be inspirational speakers for autism awareness.

CHAPTER 38

PROTECTIVENESS

Siblings are often overprotective and will fight anyone who makes fun of their sibling with autism. This can result in physical fights with peers or strangers who make fun of or ridicule their sibling. On the other hand, some siblings shy away or get embarrassed when someone is making fun of their sibling with autism and don't speak up in fear of getting bullied themselves.

Oftentimes when I was younger, I didn't stand up for my brother when he was getting picked on for fear of being bullied myself. I regret that decision to this day. Later, when people from my school were making fun of my brother, I stood up for my brother like a good sister should. I also told the principal of the school my situation with bullying and asked how we could solve it. People still make fun of my brother, but I will stand up for him no matter what.

CHAPTER 39

STRESS MANAGEMENT

Most siblings of people with autism have stress at home, and they should use stress-management techniques often. Here are a few ways to releases your stress:

- Read a book.
- Go for a run.
- Go hang out with your friends.
- Go to the mall and treat yourself to new clothes and accessories.
- Try hydro, art and music therapy.
- Put on calming music and relax your mind.

CHAPTER 40

VIOLENCE

Between the ages of 3 and 18, individuals diagnosed with ASD can become violent and aggressive. There may be times when your autistic sibling will get very violent and may even hurt you. Remember—your sibling doesn't want to hurt you, but autism is more powerful than they can control.

Your sibling may have a meltdown and try to hit and throw objects at you. It's best to stay out of the situation and let your parents handle it. They don't want you to risk getting hurt as well. If your sibling is out of control and can't calm down, it's best to call the police or the crisis line for assistance.

If your sibling is harming you, you and your parents should make a safety plan. There are a variety of safety plans to choose from, including the following:

- Go to the house of a family member who lives close to you until your sibling calms down and is not a threat to you anymore.
- Go to your room. You'll need to have a lock for your door so your sibling can't come in and try to harm you.
- Exit the house if you can. Go for a walk, but remember to bring your cell phone so your parents know where you are.
- Go to a friend's or neighbour's house. Explain the situation, and surely they will let you stay until it is safe to go back home.

CHAPTER 41

MOOD DISORDERS

There are many psychiatric problems associated with siblings of people with autism. Research shows that they have trouble with memory, attention, language and learning, even if they don't have autism. It might be because their mind and attention are always on their sibling and their sibling's well-being.

Research has found that the risk for neurodevelopmental conditions has increased in individuals who have a sibling with autism. Siblings are also at high risk for schizophrenia and other mental health problems. If you are experiencing mental health problems, get help immediately or go to your local health care center.

CHAPTER 42

HOW TO HELP

There are many ways to help a sibling of a child who has autism. The more support we give to siblings, the less alone they will feel. Try the following:

- Be there for them and encourage them to talk about their feelings.
- Help them form a stronger bond with their sibling.
- Help them get a better understanding of autism.
- Understand the behaviour of children with autism.
- Use stress management techniques with siblings.

CHAPTER 43

TIPS

Here are some random tips and helpful advice for siblings of people with autism:

- Sibs.org is a website for brothers and sisters of disabled children and adults. It provides support siblings no matter their age and lets you share and read personal stories.
- Go to your nearest autism services to get help from workers there.
- Read books and siblings' guides to autism to gain a better understanding.
- Help your parents around the house so they can focus more on your sibling.

CHAPTER 44

WHAT'S IT LIKE HAVING A SIBLING WITH AUTISM?

From a personal point of view, I can say that having a sibling with autism is very difficult, but it can make you see the world differently. My sibling made me understand autism more and recognize that every child with autism is not the same. I am not very patient with other people because all my patience and energy go to my sibling, but I also get annoyed with my sibling like many other people do as well.

I don't want sympathy for having an autistic brother, but I do want you to understand that it is very hard growing up with a special needs sibling. Still, I wouldn't trade him for anything. There are stressful times with having an autistic sibling, and with that can come tears, frustration and anger. Just like all humans, my sibling is unique and special.

MESSAGE FROM
THE AUTHOR

I have an autistic brother who I love dearly. When I was 3 years old and my brother was 2, my family knew there was something wrong with him. He didn't say a word, had high aggression levels and had difficulty eating. When we took him to the doctor, he sent us to go see an autism specialist about the issue. They asked about his behaviours and took notes, and he was diagnosed with autism spectrum disorder.

At that time, my parents did not know what autism was and what to think about it. Later on, they found out it was a mental condition. Over the years, my brother's autism certainly has made my family's life more stressful. I will continue to support him as long as I live, however, and I will never give up hope.

ABOUT THE AUTHOR

Sarah Yasini is originally from Oakville, Ontario. She is an autism advocate and volunteers at many autism societies and services. She is studying at McMaster University and aspires to be a cardiologist.

Printed in the United States
By Bookmasters